INTERNATIONAL CENTRE FOR MECHANICAL SCIENCES

COURSES AND LECTURES No. 145

GYULA KATONA
MATHEMATICAL INSTITUTE
HUNGARIAN ACADEMY OF SCIENCES, BUDAPEST

COMBINATORIAL SEARCH PROBLEMS

LECTURES HELD AT THE DEPARTMENT
FOR AUTOMATION AND INFORMATION
JUNE 1972

UDINE 1972

SPRINGER-VERLAG WIEN GMBH

This work is subject to copyright.

All rights are reserved,

whether the whole or part of the material is concerned

specifically those of translation, reprinting, re-use of illustrations,

broadcasting, reproduction by photocopying machine

or similar means, and storage in data banks.

© 1972 by Springer-Verlag Wien
Originally published by Springer-Verlag Wien-New York in 1972

ISBN 978-3-211-81169-6   ISBN 978-3-7091-4317-9 (eBook)
DOI 10.1007/978-3-7091-4317-9

PREFACE

Inspector Maigret has usually the following situation. He has a finite set of suspects, and by different methods he has to find the only (suppose there is only one) perpetrator. However, sometimes the situation of a physician is similar: he has to find the only desease of the patient from the finite (?) set of diseases. There are many cases when we have to find one (or more) element of a given finite set, and we want to minimize the number of necessary steps. These lecture notes give a survey of the mathematical theory of such problems. The theory is called search theory and it is a relatively new branch of the information theory. In these lecture notes the combinatorial aspects of the search theory are emphasized.

The lecture notes contain the lectures given by the author at the CISM in Udine (Summer, 1972) and they are similar to a paper of the author appearing in the Proceedings of the Fort Collins Meetings on Combinatorics.

(Please do not loose this book, because the search theory does not give any advise how to find it.)

Udine, June 20, 1972   Gyula O.H. Katona

1. INTRODUCTION

The basic problem is the following: <u>We have a finite set</u> $X = \{x_1,...,x_n\}$ <u>and we want to identify an unknown element</u> x_i <u>of</u> X <u>testing some subset</u> A <u>of</u> X <u>whether</u> A <u>contains</u> x_i <u>or not</u>.

There are many practical problems of this type. The first one (known from mathematical problems) is the following (see Dorfman (1943) and Sterrett (1953)):

1. <u>"Wasserman-type" blood test</u> of a large population. X is the set of some men. The test may be divided conveniently into two parts: 1. A sample of blood is from every man. 2. The blood sample is subjected to a laboratory analysis which reveals the presence or absence of "syphilitic antigen". The presence of syphilitic antigen is a good indication of infection, for the second step instead of carrying out the test individually we can pour together some samples. Carrying out the second step on the mixture we may determine, whether the given subset of men contains an infected man or not.

2. <u>Diagnosis of a sick TV set</u>. X is the set of parts of the TV set. First we see there is a good picture. The trouble must be in the "sound channel", which is a subset of the set of the parts of the TV set. Similarly, by different tests we

can determine whether certain subsets contain the ill part or not.

3. <u>Chemical analysis</u>. Assume we have an unknown chemical element and we want to identify it. X is the set of the chemical elements. We pour some chemical to the unknown one, if its colour will be red we know it belongs to a subset of the set of chemical elements. In the contrary case it does not belong. After carrying out some such tests we can identify the unknown element.

4. <u>Defective coin problem</u>. X consists of 27 coins, one of them is defective. The defective coin is heavier than the good ones. We have an equal arm balance, and we want to identify the defective coin by weighings. If we put on the balance two sets of coins of equal size, then we can see which one contains the defective coin, and if they are equally heavy then the remaining set must contain it. In the previous examples we divided the set X into two subsets (A and its complement X-A). However, in this case we divide X into three disjoint subsets, and after the weighing we know which one contains the unknown defec̲tive coin. Thus, this problem belongs to a generalization of the original problem.

The above examples differ in many things.

(A) (α) In the 3rd and 4th (and probably in the 2nd) example there is exactly one unknown defective (*) element.

(*) Sometimes we say briefly "unknown element" or "unknown".

Classification of models

(β) In the 1st example the elements may be infected independently with equal probability. It may occur that all the persons are infected or that all of them are healthy.

(B) In these examples the next subset may be (α) dependent or (β) independent on the answers of the previous tests. If the person or the machine performing the tests has a sufficiently large memory, then it may depend on the answers; in the contrary case it may not.

(C) (α) In the 1st example we may choose any subsets for test, (β) however, in the cases of the 2nd, 3rd and 4th examples the electrical construction, the chemical properties and the condition that two subsets of three parts are equally sized, produce restrictions for choosing sets.

(D) (α) In the 1st, 2nd and 3rd examples we test a subset of X ; in other words we divide X into two subsets (into A and $X-A$). The answer says which one contains the (or an) unknown element.

(β) In the 4th example we divide into three parts. Practically, in the 3rd example we always divide into many parts; pouring the testing chemical we can get many different colours. From the colour we may determine to which subset the unknown element belongs. The number of subsets may change from step to step.

(E) Our aim (in all cases) is to minimize either (α) the average number of tests, or (β) the maximal number of tests.

There are many other different questions. We do not want to list all of them frightening away the reader. We shall investigate some of them at later paragraphs. There is one more reassuring fact: We do not know the solutions of all the problems obtained by combination of the cases of (A), (B), (C) and (D).

We shall not investigate three kinds of problems: 1. the method "element by element"; p_i is the probability of x_i being wrong, c_i is the cost of the test of x_i, determine the optimal order of the tests, 2. the case in which X is infinite, 3. sequential decoding of information theory. Problem 1 has no combiantorial aspects, problem 2 has some, but its methods are rather analytical. Finally, Problem 3 has some connections with problems treated in this survey paper; however, these problems are very involved and the connections are not clear yet.

Let us first examine (for warming up) a trivial case $(A\alpha), (B\beta), (C\alpha), (D\alpha), (E\alpha) = (E\beta)$. We have a finite set $X = \{x_1, \ldots, x_n\}$ and exactly one unknown element x_i. We have to determine a family $A_1, \ldots, A_m$ of subsets in such a way, that

(1.1) after knowing whether $A_1, \ldots, A_m$ contains x_i or not we can determine x_i.

$(B\beta)$ means that we test all A_j's independently of the answers, $(C\alpha)$ means we can use any subset of X for A_i's. The number of the tests does not depend on the unknown element x_i. It is m. Thus, we have to minimize m under the condition (1.1), where A_j's run over all the subsets of X.

Put $B_j^1 = A_j$ and $B_j^2 = X - A_j$ $(1 \leq j \leq m)$.
If we know whether A_j $(1 \leq j \leq m)$ contains x_i or not, we also know whether $B_1^{i_1} B_2^{i_2} \ldots B_m^{i_m}$ $(i_1, \ldots, i_m = 1$ or $2)$ contains x_i or not. These sets are disjoint for different sequences $i_1, \ldots, i_m$. Conversely, if we know which $B_1^{i_1} \ldots B_m^{i_m}$ contains x_i, then we know whether A_j $(1 \leq j \leq m)$ contains x_i or not (depending on i_j). Thus, (1.1) is equivalent with the condition that

$$B_1^{i_1} B_2^{i_2} \ldots B_m^{i_m} \text{ contains at most 1 element for each } i_1, \ldots, i_m, \quad (1.2)$$

and if we write $i_j = 1$ if $x_i \in A_j$ and $i_j = 2$ if $x_i \notin A_j$ then $B_1^{i_1} \ldots B_m^{i_m}$ is the unknown element.

Moreover (1.2) is equivalent to the following condition:

For each pair x_j, x_k $(j \neq k)$ there is an A_l such that

$$x_j \in A_l \quad \text{and} \quad x_k \notin A_l$$

or (1.3)

$$x_j \notin A_l \quad \text{and} \quad x_k \in A_l.$$

Indeed, if (1.3) does not hold, then $x_j \in B_l^i$ and $x_k \in B_l^i$ are satisfied at the same time ($i = 1$ or 2). Choosing $i_1, \ldots, i_m$ in such a way that $x_j \in B_1^{i_1} \ldots B_m^{i_m}$, it has another element x_k in contradiction with (1.2). Conversely, if (1.2) does not hold, then for some x_j, x_k ($j \neq k$) and $i_1, \ldots, i_m$ we have $x_j, x_k \in B_1^{i_1} \ldots B_m^{i_m}$. In this case $x_j \notin B_l^{i_l}$ and $x_k \in B_l^{i_l}$, that is, $x_j \in A_l$ and $x_k \in A_l$ hold at the same time ($1 \leq l \leq m$) in contradiction with (1.3).

We call a family of subsets $A_1, \ldots, A_m$ <u>separating system</u> if they satisfy either (1.1) or (1.2) or (1.3).

There is a 4th characterization of separating systems. Define the 0,1 matrix $M = (a_{ij})$ in the following way.

$$a_{ij} = 1 \quad \text{iff} \quad x_j \in A_i \quad (1 \leq i \leq m, \; 1 \leq j \leq n)$$

Then (1.3) is equivalent to:

(1.4)   M has different columns

After these preliminary remarks our first mathematical problem becomes very easy: <u>Given n, determine the minimal m such that there exists an $m \times n$ matrix with different columns</u>. The number of different columns is 2^m, thus $2^m \geq n$ necessarily holds. In other words $m \geq \log n$. (We shall always use logarithm with basis 2) or $m \geq \{\log n\}$ where $\{x\}$ denotes the least integer $\geq x$. This estimation is the best possible: choosing n columns arbitrarily from the different $2^{\{\log n\}}$ 0,1 sequences we obtain a good matrix M.

<u>Theorem 1</u>. <u>If X is a finite set of n elements, then the minimal separating system consists of $\{\log n\}$ elements</u>.

2. CONNECTIONS WITH NOISELESS ENCODING

Restrict ourselves now for the case $(A\alpha),(B\alpha),(C\alpha),(D\alpha),(E\alpha)$.

We have again a finite set $X = \{x_1,\ldots,x_n\}$; exactly one element x_i of X is defective (wrong, unknown) with probabilities $p_1,\ldots,p_n$. Further, there are subsets $A_1, A_j(e_1,\ldots,e_{j-1})$ where A_1 is the first test, and $A_j(e_1,\ldots,e_{j-1})$ ($1 \le j \le m$; $e_1,\ldots,e_{j-1} = 0$ or 1) is the j-th test when the answer of the previous tests were $e_1,\ldots,e_{j-1}$ ($e_k = 1$ means: it contains x_i; $e_k = 0$ means: it does not contain x_i).

If $A_{l+1}(e_1,\ldots,e_l)$ is not defined, but $A_l(e_1,\ldots,e_{l-1})$ does, then the answers $e_1,\ldots,e_{l-1},e_l$ (together with the subsets $A_1, A_2(e_1),\ldots, A_k(e_1,\ldots,e_{l-1})$) uniquely determine x_i.

(2.5)

We call such a family of subsets a <u>strategy</u>.

If we fix x_i for a moment, then the sequence $e_1(i),\ldots,e_{l_i}(i)$ of answers is uniquely determined ($(A_{l_i+1}(e_1(i),\ldots,e_{l_i}(i))$ is not defined). The number of necessary test is l_i. The average number of tests is

$$\sum_{i=1}^{n} p_i l_i \qquad (2.6)$$

2. Connections with noiseless encoding

We have to minimize (2.6) over the strategies, where A's run over all the subsets of X.

Observe that in this way we corresponded a 0,1 sequence $e_1(i), \ldots, e_{l_i}(i)$ with every x_i. This is a <u>code</u> in the language of information theory. The sequences are called codewords. This code has a simple property: There are no two different i and j such that $l_j \geq l_i$ and

$$e_1(i) = e_1(j), \ldots, e_{l_i}(i) = e_{l_i}(j).$$

In other words, no codeword is a <u>segment</u> of another one. We say that it is a <u>prefix code</u>.

This definition is adopted for the case when we use codewords formed from r different symbols $y_1, \ldots, y_r$ instead of 0 and 1.

Conversely, if we have a prefix code $x_i \to e_1(i), \ldots, e_{l_i}(i)$ formed from 0's and 1's, then we can define a strategy in the following way

$$A_1 = \{x_i : e_1(i) = 1\}$$

(2.7) $\quad A_j(e_1, \ldots, e_{j-1}) = \{x_i : e_1(i) = e_1, \ldots, e_{j-1}(i) = e_{j-1}, e_j(i) = 1\}$

$$(j > 1)$$

where $e_1, \ldots, e_{j-1}$ is a fixed sequence of 0's and 1's. If the set in the right hand side is empty, we do not define $A_j(e_1, \ldots, e_{j-1})$. For any fixed x_i we get the results $e_1(i), \ldots, e_{l_i}(i)$, writing 1 if the testing subset contains x_i and 0 if not. (It is easy to see by induction.) After these l_i tests x_i uniquely defined by the prefix property of the code. Thus (2.7) is a strategy and we found a correspondence between the prefix codes and the strategies, moreover this correspondence is length-preserving: the length of the codeword of x_i is equal to the number of tests necessary to identify x_i.

This correspondence was described by Sobel (1960), (cf. Section 12), by Picard (1965) and by Campbell (1968), and it may also have been known to earlier authors. However, the optimal strategies do not coincide as Sobel (1967) has noticed in his Appendix. He investigates this connection in another paper (1970), too.

This correspondence allows us to use the following well known theorem of information theory:

<u>Noiseless Coding Theorem.</u> <u>If the symbols $x_1, \ldots, x_n$ are encoded by the symbols $y_1, \ldots, y_m$ in a prefix way, then</u>

$$L = \sum_{i=1}^{n} p_i l_i \geq \frac{-\sum_{i=1}^{n} p_i \log p_i}{\log m} = \frac{H(P)}{\log m} \quad (2.8)$$

<u>where</u> $P = (p_1, \ldots, p_n)$ $(p_i > 0, \Sigma p_i = 1)$ <u>is the vector of probabilities of the symbols</u> $x_1, \ldots, x_n$ <u>and</u> l_i <u>is the length of the codeword of</u> x_i.

<u>On the other hand, we can always find a prefix code satisfying the inequality</u>

2. Connections with noiseless encoding

$$(2.9) \qquad L \leq \frac{H(P)}{\log m} + 1 .$$

We do not prove it here. The reader can find it in any information-theoretical book (e.g. Feinstein (1958)).

Substituting $m = 2$ this theorem gives us good estimates for the minimum of the average test-number:

$$(2.10) \qquad H(P) \leq L \leq H(P) + 1 .$$

However, it remains an open question what is the exact minimum. To answer this question let us examine some simple properties of the (in average sense) shortest code. Assume $p_1 \geq \ldots \geq p_n$.

Lemma 1. For the optimal prefix code $l_1 \leq \ldots \leq l_n$.

Proof. If there is a pair i, j such that $p_i > p_j$ and $l_i > l_j$, then changing the code words of x_i and x_j the average increases by $p_i l_j + p_j l_i - p_i l_i - p_j l_j = (p_i - p_j)(l_j - l_i)$ and this is negative. The lemma is proved.

Lemma 2. If $l_i = l_n$, then $e_1(i), \ldots, e_{l_i-1}(i)$, $1 - e_{l_i}(i)$ is also a code word together with $e_1(i), \ldots, e_{l_i-1}(i)$, $e_{l_i}(i)$.

Proof. In the contrary case change the code word $e_1(i), \ldots, e_{l_i}(i)$ for $e_1(i), \ldots, e_{l_i-1}(i)$. The new word can not be a segment of an other one (the only possibilities $e_1(i), \ldots, e_{l_i}(i)$ and $e_1(i), \ldots, 1 - e_{l_i}(i)$ are excluded). Conversely, any segment of the new code word is a segment of $e_1(i), \ldots, e_{l_i}(i)$ and this is impossible by the prefix property. Thus, the new code is prefix, too. The average code length is smaller; this is a contradiction. The proof is completed.

Denote by $L(p_1, \ldots, p_n)$ the average code length $\Sigma p_i l_i$ for a given code, and by $L_{min}(p_1, \ldots, p_n)$ its minimum for prefix codes. Let us consider a code with average code length $L_{min}(p_1, \ldots, p_n)$. By lemma 1 x_n has a code of maximal length: $e_1(n), \ldots, e_{l_n}(n)$. If we change its last element, then the new sequence is a code word, too:

$$(e_1(n), \ldots, 1-e_{l_n}(n)) = (e_1(i), \ldots, e_{l_n}(i)) \qquad (i \neq n).$$

Here $l_i = l_n$, thus, again by Lemma 1 $l_i = l_{n-1} = l_n$. Changing the code words of x_i and x_{n-1} the average code length does not change; we may assume $i = n-1$. Let us omit the code words of x_{n-1} and x_n and take a new one for both of them: $e_1(n), \ldots, e_{l_n-1}(n)$. This code is prefix again, and its average code length is smaller by $p_{n-1} + p_n$.

$$L_{min}(p_1, \ldots, p_n) = L(p_1, \ldots, p_{n-1} + p_n) + p_{n-1} + p_n.$$

Hence
(2.11)
$$L_{min}(p_1, \ldots, p_n) \geq L_{min}(p_1, \ldots, p_{n-1} + p_n) + p_{n-1} + p_n$$

follows. On the other hand if it is given a code with average code length $L_{min}(p_1, \ldots, p_{n-1} + p_n)$ then we can form a new prefix code writing 0 and 1 at the end of the code word with probability $p_{n-1} + p_n$. The average code length is enlarged by $p_{n-1} + p_n$:

(2.12) $\quad L_{min}(p_1, \ldots, p_n) \leq L_{min}(p_1, \ldots, p_{n-1} + p_n) + p_{n-1} + p_n$.

(2.11) and (2.12) result in

(2.13) $\quad L_{min}(p_1, \ldots, p_n) = L_{min}(p_1, \ldots, p_{n-1} + p_n) + p_{n-1} + p_n$.

We have the following important result:

Theorem 2. We reach the optimal code with the following Huffman procedure: Assume that a code with average code length $L_{min}(p_1, \ldots, p_{n-1} + p_n)$ is determined, where p_{n-1} and p_n are the two smallest probabilities. Write 0 and 1 at the end of the code word with probability $p_{n-1} + p_n$. This is the optimal code for $P = (p_1, \ldots, p_n)$. The optimal code for $P=(1)$ is the void sequence.

The theorem was first proved by Huffman (1952), but it was independently found by Zimmerman (1959) in the language of search.

A simple example:

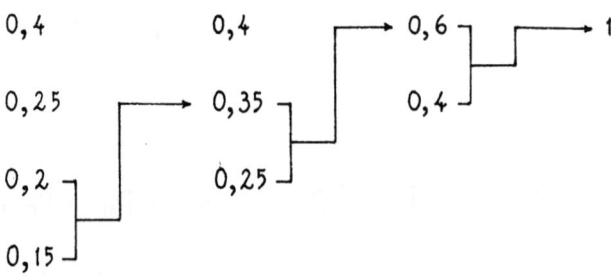

The code for $(0,6 ; 0,4)$ is $0,1$.

Differences from coding theory 17

The code for $(0,4\,;\,0,35\,;\,0,25)$ is 1, 00, 1 .

The code for $(0,4\,;\,0,25\,;\,0,2\,;\,0,15)$ is 1, 01, 000, 001 .

Theorem 2 gives us the answer for our question. The next question arises: Is there any difference between search theory and noiseless code theory? The answer is clear: there are many differences.

1. Code theory does not give solution for the problems of type $(A\beta)$ or, in general, for the problems where there are two unknown elements with positive probability.

2. In the case of $(C\beta)$ the possible restrictions for the testing subsets give restriction for the corresponding codes. However, these restrictions are different from the usual restrictions of the code theory.

3. Perhaps the most important difference is, that at a noiseless channel we have many symbols to transmit. Thus, we consider the sequences of length N formed from $x_1,\ldots,x_n$ and we transmit these sequences as new symbols. By this method we may approximate the lower bound of (2.10) arbitrarily good. The Huffman-procedure has less interest in this case. However, in the case of search we have usually only one set and one unknown. Here the Huffman-procedure has a great interest, too.

In any case, if the code theorems do not give the exact solution of a search problem, they give (sometimes good) estimates.

We have to mention that in the case when

we can divide the set by one test into m subsets, then we can also use the noiseless coding theorem and a modified form of Huffman-procedure.

3. RESULTS

$$(A\alpha)(B\alpha)(C\alpha)(D\alpha)(E\alpha)$$

After these long preliminaries we start the real survey of results.

First consider the following problem: Just one of the elements $x_1,\ldots,x_n$ is defective with equal probability. What is the minimum of the average number of tests necessary to identify the defective element. This problem is obviously a particular case of the problem treated in the previous section. Theorem 2 gives an algorithm to determine $L_{min}\left(\frac{1}{n},\ldots,\frac{1}{n}\right)$, however in this special case we may determine the exact value.

Lemma 3. <u>The code words of the code having average length $L_{min}\left(\frac{1}{n},\ldots,\frac{1}{n}\right)$ can have just two different lengths, which are consecutive integers.</u>

<u>Proof</u>. Assume $l_1 \leq \ldots \leq l_n$. If $l_1 \leq l_n - 2$ then consider the code word $e_1(n),\ldots,e_{l_n}(n)$. By Lemma 2 there exists a code word of the form $e_1(n),\ldots,1 - e_{l_n}(n)$. Change the code words

$e_1(n),\ldots,e_{l_n-1}(n), e_{l_n}(n)$ for $e_1(n),\ldots,e_{l_n-1}(n)$

$e_1(n),\ldots,e_{l_n-1}(n), 1 - e_{l_n}(n)$ for $e_1(1),\ldots,e_{l_1}(1), 0$

$e_1(1),\ldots,e_{l_1}(1)$ for $e_1(1),\ldots,e_{l_1}(1), 1$

It is easy to see, that the new code is prefix. However, the average code length is increased by $(2(l_1+1)+l_n-1)/n - (2l_n+l_1)/n = (l_1-l_n+1)/n$ which is negative by the assumption $l_1 \le l_n - 2$. The new code has a smaller average length. This is a contradiction. We proved $l_1 \ge l_n - 1$. The proof is completed.

Choosing an arbitrary 0,1 sequence $c_1, \ldots, c_{l_n-1}$ of length $l_n - 1$, either, it is a code word or one of the sequences

(3.14)
$$e_1, \ldots, e_{l_n-1}, 0$$
$$e_1, \ldots, e_{l_n-1}, 1$$

in a code word. In the contrary case we would change a code word of length l_n for $c_1, \ldots, c_{l_n-1}$ preserving the prefix property and decreasing the average length. This is a contradiction. However, by Lemma 2 if one of the sequences (3.14) is a code word then the second one is also a code word. Thus either $e_1, \ldots, e_{l_n-1}$ or both (3.14) are code words. Denoting by s the number of code words of length $l_n - 1$ we have

(3.15)
$$s + \frac{n+s}{2} = 2^{l_n-1}$$

Here $0 \le s < n$, and $\frac{n}{2} \le \frac{n+s}{2}$
Using (3.15) we obtain the inequality

$$\frac{n}{2} \le 2^{l_n-1} < n$$

or $\log n \leq l_n < \log n + 1$. It results in $l_n = \{\log n\}$ where $\{x\}$ denotes the least integer $\geq x$. On the other hand, we may count s from (3.15):

$$s = 2^{\{\log n\}} - n .$$

The average is

$$\frac{s(\{\log n\} - 1) + (n-s)\{\log n\}}{n} = \{\log n\} - \left(\frac{2^{\{\log n\}}}{n} - 1\right) .$$

Theorem 3.

$$L_{min}\left(\frac{1}{n}, \ldots, \frac{1}{n}\right) = \{\log n\} - \left(\frac{2^{\{\log n\}}}{n} - 1\right) .$$

This theorem was proved first by Sandelius (1961). Sobel (1968b) has it also as a by-product. The proof published here is different from both that of Sandelius and that of Sobel.

By this method it is easy to see the following generalization (Katona and Lee):

Theorem 4. Let $p_1 \geq \ldots \geq p_n$ be the given probabilities where $p_{n-1} + p_n \geq p_1$. Then

$$L_{min}(p_1, \ldots, p_n) = \{\log n\} - \sum_{i=1}^{s} p_i ,$$

where $s = 2^{\{\log n\}} - n$.

Theorem 5. If $p_1 \geq \ldots \geq p_n$ and $p_n + k p_{n-1} > p_1$

then

$$l_n - l_1 \leq k$$

that is, the number of different code lengths is at most $k+1$.

Sobel (1968b) determined an other special case:

Theorem 6. If $p_i = \dfrac{i}{\frac{n(n+1)}{2}}$ ($1 \leq i \leq n$) then for $2^{[\log n]} \leq n < 3 \cdot 2^{[\log n]-1}$ (*)

$$L_{min}(p_1, \ldots, p_n) = ([\log n] + 2) + \left(3 \cdot 2^{2[\log n]-3} - 3 \cdot 2^{[\log n]-2}(2n+1)\right) \Big/ \frac{n(n+1)}{2}$$

and for $3 \cdot 2^{[\log n]-1} \leq n < 2^{[\log n]+1}$

$$L_{min}(p_1, \ldots, p_n) = ([\log n] + 2) + \left(3 \cdot 2^{2[\log n]-1} - 3 \cdot 2^{[\log n]-1}(2n+1)\right) \Big/ \frac{n(n+1)}{2}.$$

$(A\alpha)(B\alpha)(C\alpha)(D\alpha)(E\alpha)$

In this case the probabilities do not play any role. We may choose them $p_i = \dfrac{1}{n}$ ($1 \leq i \leq n$), and use Theorem 3:

$$L_{min}\left(\frac{1}{n}, \ldots, \frac{1}{n}\right) = \{\log n\} - \left(\frac{2^{\{\log n\}}}{n} - 1\right).$$

However the maximum $\geq$ the average. Denote by l the minimum of the masimal test number. Thus

(3.16) $\qquad l \geq \{\log n\} - \left(\dfrac{2^{\{\log n\}}}{n} - 1\right).$

(*) $[x]$ denotes the largest integer $\leq x$.

Here

$$1 \le \frac{2^{\{\log n\}}}{n} < 2$$

and

$$\{\log n\} - \left(\frac{2^{\{\log n\}}}{n} - 1\right) > \{\log n\} - 1 . \qquad (3.17)$$

From (3.16) and (3.17) we obtain

$$l \ge \{\log n\} .$$

However by Theorem 1 we can construct a strategy even by independent tests ($(B\beta)$) with test length $\{\log n\}$.

Theorem 7. Assume we have strategies for $X = \{x_1, \ldots, x_n\}$. *The minimum (runs over strategies) of the maximal number of tests is*

$$l = \{\log n\}.$$

It is quite interesting that in the case $(A\alpha)(C\alpha)(E\beta)$ the optimality problems are equivalent for $(B\alpha)$ and $(B\beta)$; we do not obtain anything if we choose the next test depending on the answers of the previous tests.

$(A\alpha)(B\beta)(C\alpha)(D\alpha)(E\alpha) = (E\beta)$

Theorem 1 gives answer for this case.

$$(A\alpha), (B\alpha), (C\beta), (D\alpha), (E\alpha).$$

It is a very natural assumption, that a linear order $x_1 < \ldots < x_n$ is given in X, and the admissible subsets are of type $\{x_1, \ldots, x_j\}$ or $\{x_j, \ldots, x_n\}$ ($1 \le j \le n$).

For example we want to classify apples according to their sizes. $x_1, \ldots, x_n$ are the classes, and the unknown x_i is the class of the given apple. We carry out the tests by holes. If the given apple falls through the hole then for its class $x_i \in \{x_1, \ldots, x_j\}$ for some j depending on the hole. Conversely if it does not fall through, then x_i belongs to $\{x_{j+1}, \ldots, x_n\}$.

What does this restriction mean on the language of codes? The tests $\{x_1, \ldots, x_j\}$ and $\{x_{j+1}, \ldots, x_n\}$ are equivalent, assume we use always the type $\{x_{j+1}, \ldots, x_n\}$. If $A_1 = \{x_{j+1}, \ldots, x_n\}$ then for the corresponding code we have

$$e_1(1) = \ldots = e_1(j) = 0 \quad , \quad e_1(j+1) = \ldots = e_1(n) = 1 \ .$$

Similarly, if $A_k(e_1, \ldots, e_{k-1}) = \{x_{l+1}, \ldots, x_n\}$ then considering the set $T = \{t : e_1(t) = e_1, \ldots, e_{k-1}(t) = e_{k-1}\}$ we have again

$$e_k(t) = 0 \qquad t \le l \ , \quad t \in T$$

and

$$e_k(t) = 1 \qquad t > l \ , \quad t \in T \ .$$

Reformulating, it means that for any pair

$$e_1(t) = e_1(u), \ldots, e_{k-1}(t) = e_{k-1}(u), e_k(t) = 0 \ , \quad e_k(u) = 1$$

Alphabetical codes

for some k, that is the code words are in <u>lexicographic</u> order. We say that the code is <u>alphabetical</u> if it possesses this property.

Our problem is to determine the prefix alphabetical code with minimal average length. Denote this average by $A_{min}(p_1, \ldots, p_n)$.

Gilbert and Moore (1959) gave an efficient construction for alphabetical codes, which ensures the following estimation:

<u>Theorem 8.</u>

$$H(P) \leq A_{min}(p_1, \ldots, p_n) \leq H(P) + 2 , \qquad (3.18)$$

<u>where</u> $P = (p_1, \ldots, p_n)$.

<u>Proof</u>. The left hand side is a consequence of the left hand side of (2.10) and of the trivial inequality

$$L_{min}(p_1, \ldots, p_n) \leq A_{min}(p_1, \ldots, p_n). \qquad (3.19)$$

We prove the right hand side of (3.18) by a construction. Define the numbers $q_1, \ldots, q_n$ and $l_1, \ldots, l_n$ as follows:

$$q_j = \sum_{i=1}^{j-1} p_i + \frac{p_j}{2} ,$$

$$l_j = \{-\log p_j\} + 1 . \qquad (3.20)$$

Let the first l_j digits of the binary expansion of the number be the code of x_j. If the prefix property does not hold, then the code of some x_i is a segment of the code of an other x_j. It means that q_i and q_j have the same binary digits on the first l_i places. In other words

$$|q_i - q_j| \leq \frac{1}{2^{l_i}} \leq \frac{1}{2^{-\log p_i + 1}} = \frac{1}{2} p_i ,$$

and this contradicts (3.20), since

$$|q_i - q_j| \geq \frac{1}{2} p_i + \frac{1}{2} p_j > \frac{1}{2} p_i$$

The constructed code is prefix, indeed. The alphabetical property trivially satisfied. The average length is

$$\sum_{j=1}^{n} p_j l_j \leq \sum_{j=1}^{n} p_j (\{-\log p_j\} + 1) \leq$$

$$\leq \sum_{j=1}^{n} p_j (-\log p_j + 2) = H(P) + 2 .$$

The proof is completed.

Knuth, further Hu and Tucker (1970) worked out algorithms to determine a good alphabetical code.

In the paper of Hu and Tucker the <u>tentative-connecting</u> algorithm is written down. This need not be directly associated with an alphabetical code, but it is proved that there exists an alphabetical code with the same code word lengths as the code generated by the tentative-connecting algorithm.

A code is equivalent to the following tree: The nodes are the different possible segments of the code words (including the void sequence, which is called <u>root</u>), and two nodes are connected if one of them is a segment of the other, and their lengths differ one. The <u>terminal</u> nodes are the code code words. The tentative-connecting algorithm determines the tree rather than the code.

We start the algorithm with the subtree consisting of the terminal nodes $c_1, \ldots, c_n$ with the given order (no edges). Every terminal node has a weight p_j. We take the minimal sum of the form $p_j + p_{j+1}$ ($1 \le j < n$), we draw a new node d with weight $p_j + p_{j+1}$, and we connect d with c_j and c_{j+1}. We have a new subtree and a new <u>construction sequence</u>: $c_1, \ldots, c_{j-1}, d, c_{j+2}, \ldots, c_n$. In general assume we have a subtree and its roots and terminal nodes form a construction sequence $d_1, \ldots, d_k$ (some of d's are c's); they have weights $q_1, \ldots, q_k$, d_i and d_j ($i<j$) are <u>tentative connected</u> if there is no d_k ($i<k<j$) such that $d_k = c_\ell$ for some ℓ. We form the minimal sum $q_i + q_j$ where d_i and d_j are tentative connected ($i<j$). We connect the new code e with d_i and d_j. The new construction sequence is $d_1, \ldots, d_{i-1}, e, d_{i+1}, \ldots, d_{j-1}, d_{j+1}, \ldots, d_k$. The corresponding weights are

$$q_1, \ldots, q_{i-1}, q_i + q_j, q_{i+1}, \ldots, q_{j-1}, q_{j+1}, \ldots, q_k.$$

We continue this procedure until the construction sequence consists of one element.

Observe that in this language Huffman-algorithm means that we choose the minimal sum $q_i + q_j$ without any restriction.

Notice that

$$A_{min}\left(\frac{1}{n},\ldots,\frac{1}{n}\right) = L_{min}\left(\frac{1}{n},\ldots,\frac{1}{n}\right)$$

This is a consequence of the fact that in this case the average does not depend on the order.

By the methods of Lemma 3 it is easy to verify the following theorem (Katona and Lee).

<u>Theorem 9. If $p_i + p_{i+1} > p_j$ $(1 \leq i < n, 1 \leq j \leq n)$ then the minimal alphabetic code can have only two different code word lengths, which are consecutive integers.</u>

It is an interesting question how Huffman algorithm is modified if we have a prescribed bound b for the code lengths ($b > \{\log n\}$)

$$l_i \leq b \qquad (1 \leq i \leq n) \quad,$$

but we are interested in the minimal average length. Cesari (1968) has a partial solution for the problem.
$(A\alpha)(B\alpha)(C\beta)(D\alpha)(E\beta)$.

In this case the solutions of the problems of the

Restriction on the sizes of the subsets

last section are trivial and identical to Theorem 7.

However, there are other problems which are too difficult in the case of $(E\alpha)$.

Let us have n coins $x_1, \ldots, x_n$ one of them is defective (say x_i). The weight w_j of a non-defective coin is

$$1 \leq w \leq 1 + \delta$$

and $w_i = 1 + \varepsilon$ $(\varepsilon > \delta)$. We can use scales (not equal arm balance), thus by one test we may determine the weight of a subset A of $\{x_1, \ldots, x_n\}$. If the number $|A|$ of elements of A is less than $\left[\frac{\varepsilon}{\delta}\right]$, then $x_i \in A$ if and only if the weight of the subset A is $\geq |A| + \varepsilon$, because in the contrary case its weight is less than $|A| + \delta \left[\frac{\varepsilon}{\delta}\right] \leq$
$\leq |A| + \varepsilon$.

This example raises the following problem. It is given a finite set $X = \{x_1, \ldots, x_n\}$. Determine the minimum of the maximal test number for strategies consisting of subsets of at most k elements (k is fixed $\leq n$).

Denote by $f_k(n)$ this minimum. We know from Theorem 7 that

$$f_k(n) \geq \{\log n\}.$$

If $k \geq \frac{n}{2}$ we do not have an essential restriction by $|A| \leq k$, for instead of $|A| > k$ we can use the complement $X - A$, where $|X - A| < n - k \leq k$. Thus, by Theorem 7

(3.21) $\qquad f_k(n) = \{\log n\} \qquad$ if $\qquad \left[\frac{n}{2}\right] \leq k$

Assume now $\frac{n}{2} > k$. It is clear that $f_k(n)$ is a monotonically increasing function of n. Suppose for the optimal strategy $|A_1| = l$ $(1 \leq l \leq k)$ holds. If the subsets $A_j(e_1, \ldots, e_{j-1})$ form a strategy, then $A_1 \cap A_j(e_1, \ldots, e_{j-1})$ and $(X-A_1) \cap A_j(e_1, \ldots, e_{j-1})$ form a strategy on A_1 and $X - A_1$, respectively. Similarly $|A_j(e_1, \ldots, e_{j-1})| \leq k$ results in $|A_1 \cap A_j(e_1, \ldots, e_{j-1})| \leq k$ and

$$|(X - A_1) \cap A_j(e_1, \ldots, e_{j-1})| \leq k$$

For these strategies the maximal number of test is at least $f_k(l)$ and $f_k(n-l)$, respectively. We have the following inequality

(3.22) $\qquad f_k(n) \geq 1 + \max(f_k(l) + f_k(n-l))$

Here $l \leq n-l$ by $l \leq k$ and $k < \frac{n}{2}$. Applying the monotonicity of $f_k(n)$ we have

(3.23) $\qquad \max(f_k(l), f_k(n-l)) = f_k(n-l)$

and

(3.24) $\qquad f_k(n-l) \geq f_k(n-k)$.

Substitute (3.23) and (3.24) into (3.22):

(3.25) $\qquad f_k(n) \geq 1 + f_k(n-k)$.

Restriction on the sizes of the subsets

Applying $v = \{\frac{n}{k}\} - 2$ times (3.25)

$$f_k(n) \geq v + f_k(n - kv)$$

follows. Here $n - kv \leq 2k$ is trivial, for the last term we can apply (3.21)

$$f_k(n) \geq v + \{\log(n - kv)\}.$$

However, it is easy to construct a strategy with this maximal test number. $A_1 = \{x_1, \ldots, x_k\}$, $A_2 = \{x_{k+1}, \ldots, x_{2k}\}, \ldots, A_v = \{x_{(v-1)k-1}, \ldots, x_{vk}\}$ are the first v tests. They are independent from the previous answers. After these tests we know that either $x_i \in A_j$ for some j $(1 \leq j \leq v)$ or $x_i \in \{x_{vk+1}, \ldots, x_n\}$. In the first case we have a strategy with maximal length $\{\log k\}$ to identify x_i by Theorem 7. In the second case we have a strategy with $\{\log(n - kv)\}$. Here $n - kv > k$, and the maximal length is $v + \{\log(n - kv)\}$. The conjecture of Vigassy is proved:

Theorem 10. <u>The minimum of the maximal test number of a strategy given to identify one of the n elements is $\{n/k\} - 2 + \{\log(n - k(\{n/k\} - 2))\}$ if the subsets used on the strategy can have at most k elements $(k < n)$.</u>

The next problem is a typical problem of computers. <u>There are given n numbers $y_1, \ldots, y_n$ whose values are unknown and pairwise unequal. We wish to order them using only binary comparisons.</u>

In other words we have an unknown permutation x_i

from all the permutations $x_1, \ldots, x_{n!}$ of $y_1, \ldots, y_n$. The subsets we can use for tests consist of the permutations where y_i precedes y_j (for some fixed i and j ($i \neq j$)). There are $n!$ permutations, thus, by Theorem 7 the minimum of the maximal test number is

(3.26) $$l \geq \log(n!).$$

Steinhaus (1950) proposed the following algorithm: Assume we have already ordered $y_1, \ldots, y_t$. We compare y_{t+1} first with $y_{\{t/2\}}$, secondly with $y_{\{t/4\}}$ or $y_{\{3t/4\}}$ depending on the answer of the first test, and so on ... . The number of test is maximally

(3.27) $$l \leq \{\log 2\} + \{\log 3\} \ldots + \{\log(n-1)\} < \log((n-1)!) + n - 3.$$

Steinhaus conjectured in (1950) this procedure to be optimal, however in (1958) he disproved the conjecture. Asymptotically, the lower ((3.26)) and the upper ((3.27)) bounds are equivalent, but we do not know the best algorithm up to now. Ford and Johnson (1959) determined an algorithm better than Steinhaus's one. (See also Wells (1965), and Cesari (1968)).

A generalization of the above problem is to find and order the t largest y's. This generalization does not belong to the general search problem treated here. But we can generalize it toward this direction: <u>The n objects $x_1, \ldots, x_n$ are divided into disjoint classes. We wish to determine just the class to which the unknown x_i belongs.</u>

In our case: $x_1, \ldots, x_n$ are the permutations of

$y_1, \ldots, y_n$. The classes consist of the permutations where the last t elements are fixed. The number of classes is $n(n-1) \ldots (n-t+1)$.

If $t=1$ it is easy to see that

$$l = n - 1.$$

The case $t = 2$ has been solved by Schreier (1932), Slupecki (1949-51) and Sobel (1968a). The case of general t is obviously unsolved. For estimations see Hadian and Sobel (1970). A further considered but unsolved problem is to determine the minimax of binary comparisons sufficient to identify the t-th largest element from $y_1, \ldots, y_n$. Kislicyn (1964), Hadian and Sobel (1969), and Hadian (1969) worked out algorithms.

R.C. Bose and Nelson (1961) modified the Steinhaus's problem: We wish to determine the natural order of the given (pairwise different) numbers $y_1, \ldots, y_n$ by binary changes instead of binary comparisons. That is, if $y_i < y_j$ $(i \neq j)$ there is no change, if $y_i > y_j$, we use the order $y_1, \ldots, y_{i-1}, y_j, y_{i+1}, \ldots, y_{j-1}, y_i, y_{j+1}, \ldots, y_n$. What is the minimum of the maximal number of steps needed to determine the natural order?

The minimum is not known, but a good algorithm is given by R.C. Bose and Nelson (1961). About the ordering problems see also David (1959) and Moon (1968).

$$(A\alpha)(B\beta)(C\beta)(D\alpha)(E\alpha) = (E\beta).$$

We have to determine the minimal m for which there exist subsets $A_1,\ldots,A_m$ of $X = \{x_1,\ldots,x_n\}$ constituting a strategy and satisfying $|A_i| \leq k$ ($k < \frac{n}{2}$). If the subsets of a strategy do not depend on the previous answers, then they form simply a separating system (see Introduction). It is proved by Katona (1966) that this minimal m is equal to the minimal m such that there exist non-negative integers $s_0,\ldots,s_m$ satisfying

(3.28)
$$mk = \sum_{j=0}^{m} j\, s_j$$
$$n = \sum_{j=0}^{m} s_j$$
$$s_j \leq \binom{m}{j} \qquad (0 \leq j \leq m).$$

By this fact it was proved the next

<u>Theorem 11.</u> <u>Suppose that $A_1,\ldots,A_m \subset X = \{x_1,\ldots,x_n\}$ satisfy the condition $|A_j| \leq k$ ($1 \leq j \leq m$) (k is given $< \frac{n}{2}$) and constitute a separating system. Under this condition for the minimum of m the inequalities</u>

$$\frac{\log n}{\log(en/k)} \cdot \frac{n}{k} \leq \min\ m \leq \left\{\frac{\log 2n}{\log(n/k)}\right\} \frac{n}{k}$$

<u>hold.</u>

Dickson (1969) introduced the concept of the completely separating system. (It does not have, probably, nice interpretation in search theory, but it is interesting in itself): $A_1, \ldots, A_m$ is a <u>completely separating system</u> if for any pair x_i, x_j $(i \neq j)$ there is a k such that $x_i \in A_k$, $x_j \notin A_k$.

What is the minimum of m such that there exists a completely separating system $A_1, \ldots, A_m$ for $\{x_1, \ldots, x_n\}$. It is solved by Dickson (1969) asymptotically, and Spencer (1970) proved

<u>Theorem 12.</u> <u>The minimal</u> m <u>for which a completely separating system</u> $A_1, \ldots, A_m$ <u>exist is</u>

$$\min\left\{ m : \binom{m}{\left[\frac{m}{2}\right]} \geq n \right\}$$

Two subsets A_1 and A_2 of X are said to be <u>qualitative independent</u>, if none of the sets $A_1 A_2, A_1 \bar{A}_2, \bar{A}_1 A_2, \bar{A}_1 \bar{A}_2$ is empty, where $\bar{A}$ denote the complement set $X-A$. In other words, testing first by A_1, we obtain some information by testing A_2, independently of the answer of the first test. For instance if $A_1 A_2 = \emptyset$ then after the answer $x_i \in A_1$ the test A_2 does not give any information. Rényi (1971) asked what is the maximum of the pairwise qualitative independent sets. He solved the problem for even n in the following way: If $A_1, \ldots, A_m$ are qualitative independent, then (it is easy to see) $A_1, \bar{A}_1, \ldots, A_m, \bar{A}_m$ form such a system that none of them is contained in an other one. By Sperner's theorem (1928) we obtain $2m \leq \binom{n}{\left[\frac{n}{2}\right]}$ and

$$m \le \binom{n}{\frac{n}{2}}/2.$$

This estimation is the best possible because we can choose $\binom{n}{\frac{n}{2}}/2$ pairwise disjoint subsets of $\frac{n}{2}$ elements. For odd n this estimation is not the best. The right value is

$$\binom{n-1}{\frac{n-1}{2}}$$

(see Rényi (1971)). The maximal number of r-wise qualitative independent sets is not determined yet. An estimation is given in Rényi's book (1971).

(Aβ)(Bα)(Cα)(Dα)(Eα)

Each of the elements $x_1, \ldots, x_n$ can be defective independently with probability p. We can not use the results of encoding type for this model, but it can be done for a transformed variant: Let $x'_1, \ldots, x'_{2^n}$ be the subset of $X = \{x_1, \ldots, x_n\}$. Exactly one x'_i of the elements of $X' = \{x'_1, \ldots, x'_{2^n}\}$ is "defective" (it is the subset of all defective elements). However, the testing subsets $A \subset X$ are also transformed. A has a defective element with the set x'_i of defective elements. It is equivalent to $x'_i \in A'$ where A' is the set of x_k non-disjoint to x'_j. However, such subsets A' are very special, we reduced our problem to a problem of type

(Aα)(Bα)(Cβ)(Dα)(Eα)

The restrictions for the testing subsets are very particular. We can not solve the problem, but an easy lower bound for the average number of test follows from (2.10):

$$L_{min}(P) \geq H(P)$$

where $P = (p^n, p^{n-1}q, p^{n-1}q, \ldots, q^n)$.

It is well known (see e.g. Feinstein (1958)) that $H(P) =$
$= n(-p \log p - (1-p) \log (1-p))$ holds in this case. We obtain for the average test number

$$L \geq n(-p \log p - (1-p) \log(1-p)). \qquad (3.29)$$

However, it is not the best possible lower bound. For example Ungar (1960) proved the following

Theorem 13. If $p \geq \frac{1}{3}(3-\sqrt{5})$ then

$$L \geq n$$

and for $0 \leq p \leq \frac{1}{2}(3-\sqrt{5})$ there is a strategy with

$$L < n.$$

For large p $L \geq n$ is obviously a better estimation than (3.29), and it is exact in this case, since for the strategy "element by element" $L = n$. In this case the combinatorial search fails. However, Ungar's theorem ensures that for small p it is a good method. Sobel (1960) and Sobel and Groll (1959) worked out good strategies for searching. These procedures give upper estimations for the optimal average test number $L_{min}(n)$. For example Sobel (1960) (partly personal communication) has proved

$$\lim_{n \to \infty} \frac{L_{min}(n)}{n} \leq -p\log p - q\log q + \frac{p}{1-q^x}$$

where x is the smallest integer such that $1 - q^x - q^{x+1} \geq 0$. The right hand side is $\leq p\log p - q\log q + 1$, or, if p is small, then $\leq -p\log p - q\log q + 2p$.

The next problem does not belong formally to this section, but it is a very close generalization of the problem treated here. We have 3 types of elements in X : good, mediocre and defective ones. Testing a subset A of X it shows the "minimum" of its elements: THe test says "good" if all the elements of A are good; it says "mediocre" if there is at least one mediocre element in A, but none of them is defective; it says "defective" if there is at least one defective element in A. The elements of X are good, mediocre and defective independently with probability q_1, q_2 and q_3 ($q_1 + q_2 + q_3 = 1$), respectively. Kumar (1970) has a result analogous to Ungar's theorem: If $q_1 \geq \frac{1}{2}(q_2 - 1 + (5q_2^2 - 6q_2 + 5)^{1/2})$ then $L \geq n$, that is the test "element by element" is the best possible. On the other hand, if $q_1 < \frac{1}{2}(q_2 - 1 + (5q_2^2 - 6q_2 + 5)^{1/2})$ then there is a better strategy satisfying $L = n$. Similarly, Kumar (1970) gives a good strategy, which is a generalization of Sobel (1960) and Sobel-Groll (1959).

$(A\beta)(B\alpha)(C\alpha)(D\alpha)(E\beta)$

$(A\beta)(B\beta)(C\alpha)(D\alpha)(E\alpha) = (E\beta)$

These cases are uninteresting, because for $p = \frac{1}{2}$ (3.29) gives $L \geq n$, and this is a lower bound for these cases. The strategy "element by element" is the best one.

$(A\beta)\ldots(C\beta)(D\alpha)\ldots$

These problems are not considered in the literature. Sobel (1960) is the only author that points out that his strategy is <u>alphabetical</u> in the sense that the testing subsets are "intervals" in the ordered set $\{x_1, \ldots, x_n\}$.

$(A\gamma)$

We did not introduce this notation in the first section. The common generalization of the cases $(A\alpha)$ and $(A\beta)$ is the case when the probabilities $p(A)$ of $A (\subset X)$ being the set of defective elements are given for all A.

In this generality the problem is too hard to solve. A very particular case is when $p(A) = 1/\binom{n}{2}$ for $|A| = 2$ and $0 = p(A)$ otherwise. (Assume $(B\alpha)(C\alpha)(D\alpha)(E\alpha)$). It is easy to transform it into a problem of type $(A\alpha)(B\alpha)(C\alpha)(D\alpha)(E\alpha)$ considering the set of unordered pairs (x_i, x_j) $(i \neq j)$. For this modified problem we may apply Theorem 3. More exactly, the formula of Theorem 3 gives a lower bound for minimum of the average test number. Moreover, Sobel (1968b) proved that we can reach this lower bound for infinite many n's.

<u>Theorem 14.</u> <u>There are exactly 2 defective elements in the set $\{x_1,\ldots,x_n\}$, all the possibilities with equal probabilities. For the optimal strategy the average test length is denoted by $L_2(n)$.</u>

$$L_2(n) = \{\log\binom{n}{2}\} - \left(\frac{2^{\{\log\binom{n}{2}\}}}{\binom{n}{2}} - 1\right),$$

<u>if</u> n =

$$2^{(m+1)/2} + \left[\frac{2^{(m-1)/2} - 4}{3}\right] \quad \text{for some odd} \quad m \geq 1,$$

$$2^{m/2} + \left[\frac{2^{(m+2)/2} - 4}{3}\right] \quad \text{for some even} \quad m \geq 0.$$

For the remaining n's there is a small difference between the lower bound and the average of the strategy worked out by Sobel (1968).

Sobel and Groll (1966) investigated the problem (Aβ) in the case if we do not know the exact value of p and we use an a priori distribution by the test as well as tests to get a Bayes solution of the problem. This problem is more statistical than combinatorial.

(D/β)

In this case at each test we divide X into disjoint subsets and the result of the test shows us which one (or which ones) includes the unknown element(s). If the number of disjoint subsets is at each test a constant (say r), then many problems can be solved (and they are done) in the same way as for (Dα). We do not want to repeat them.

It may occur that the number r of subsets depends on the situation, that is, on the previous tests and previous results. Picard (1965) generalized Theorem 2 (Huffman-algorithm) toward this case.

There is classical problem which belongs typically to this case: the so called "defective coin problem". The basic situation is the following one: We have n coins, one of them is defective, with probability 1. The good coins weigh 1 and the defective one weigh $1+\varepsilon$ ($0<\varepsilon<1$) We wish to find the defective coin using an equal arm balance. Let X be the set of coins. Taking a subset A and a subset B ($A \cap B = \emptyset$) on the right and left hand side of the balance, respectively, we may obtain three results: balance and unbalance in two ways. In the first case we know that the defective coin x_i is in X-A-B and in the second case we know which one of A and B includes x_i. One test divides X into 3 parts, and says which one includes x_i. However, there is a restriction: $|A| = |B|$. If we try to weigh subsets with different cardinalities, no information is obtained. (The problem belongs to case $(A\alpha)(B\alpha)(C\beta)(D\beta)(E\alpha)$ or $(E\beta)$.) Let us generalize our Theorem 3:

$$(3.30) \quad L^3_{min}\left(\frac{1}{n},\ldots,\frac{1}{n}\right) = \{\log_3 n\} - \left[\frac{3^{\{\log_3 n\}}}{2} - \frac{n}{2}\right]/n .$$

It gives a lower bound for the average test number. This lower bound is attainable even under the condition $|A|=|B|$ (see Cairns (1963) and Baranyai (a)) except for $n=6$, when the minimum of the average is 2. On the other hand, the last term in (3.30) is less than 1 (if $\{\log_3 n\} = \log_3 n$ then 0), thus $\{L^3_{min}(\frac{1}{n},\ldots,\frac{1}{n})\} = \{\log_3 n\}$ gives a lower bound for the maximal number of test sufficient to identify the defective coin.

A different problem is if in a test we can use only the elements of the subset containing the defective one according to the last test (that is we can not weigh the coins proved to be good). (3.30) is a lower bound, again.

However, because of the restriction we can not reach (3.30) for every n (for we can not reach if $3^{\{\log_3 n\}} - n \equiv 3 \pmod 4$). Cairns (1963) (for a new simpler proof see Baranyai (a)) determined the optimal strategy which is optimal for both cases $(E\alpha)$ and $(E\beta)$:

Theorem 15. The optimal strategy is the following. If we know that the defective coin is an element of an n' element subset, then let us weigh m coins against m other ones from this subset, where m is the odd one from $\left[\frac{n'+1}{3}\right]$ and $\left[\frac{n'+4}{3}\right]$. The maximum test number is $\{\log_3 n\}$ for this strategy, and the average test number is also optimal.(*)

The case when there are more (but fixed number h) defective coins is more complicated, if we assume that we are not able to determine the number of defectives in a subset by one test because the weights w_i of the defectives are different (but $1 < w_i < 1 + \frac{1}{h}$). For particular results see Cairns ($h=2$) (1963), Bellmann and Gluss (1961) and C.A.B. Smith (1947).

A different problem is proposed by Shapiro (1960) and Fine (1960). Again, we have n coins some of them are defective. The weight of good and defective ones are a and b, respectively. We may use for tests scales (not equal arm balance). Thus, by one test we are able to determine the number of defective coins in the tested subset. Determine $l(n)$, the minimum of the maximal test number needed to determine all the defectives. Many authors (Cantor (1964), Shapiro and Söderberg (1963), Erdös and Rényi (1963) have asymptotical results for $l(n)$. Finally, Lindström (1964), (1965), (1966) proved

$$\lim_{n \to \infty} \frac{l(n) \log n}{n} = 2.$$

(*) Baranyai noticed that it is not true if $n' = 3^a + 2$, the right $m = 3^{a-1}$.

4. RANDOM SEARCH

Let us go back to the simplest case: exactly one of the elements $x_1, \ldots, x_n$ is defective, x_i is defective with probability p_i. Again, subsets are used to test (any subset). Rényi proposed to choose the subset randomly, with probability $\frac{1}{2^n}$. Is the number of test much larger than in the traditional case? The answer is definitely "no" (Rényi (1962a), (1961a)):

<u>Theorem 16.</u> <u>If the subsets $A_1, \ldots, A_m$ of $X = \{x_1, \ldots, x_n\}$ are chosen independently with probability $\frac{1}{2^n}$, and $P(n,m)$ denotes the probability of the event that $A_1, \ldots, A_m$ constitute a separating system then</u>

$$\lim_{n \to \infty} P(n, 2\log n + c) = \begin{cases} 1 & \text{if } c = \infty \\ e^{-\frac{1}{2^{c+1}}} & \text{if } c \text{ is finite} \\ 0 & \text{if } c = -\infty \end{cases}$$

It means, if we choose e.g. $m = 2\log n + 6$, then for large enough n the system $A_1, \ldots, A_m$ is a separating system with probability $e^{-\frac{1}{2^7}} \sim 0,99$. Comparing with Theorem 1, choosing randomly the subsets, we have to test roughly twice as many as the minimal number of systematically selected subsets which determine uniquely the unknown element. If the costs of the tests are small and the costs of working out a systematical plan are large, then it is better to use the random search.

However, we do not need a separating system to identify the unknown x_i. It is sufficient if $A_1,\ldots,A_m$ separates x_i from the other elements, that is, if they satisfy (1.3) for x_i and for an arbitrary x_k ($1 \le k \le m, i \ne k$). Denote by $S(n,m)$ the probability of the event that $A_1,\ldots,A_m$ separates x_i (it does not depend on i).

Theorem 17. (Rényi (1962b)). If $c > 0$, then

$$S(n, \log n + c) \ge e^{-2^{-c}}$$

It means, if we use 7 more questions than at the systematical search, then we find the unknown element with probability $e^{-\frac{1}{2}^7} \sim 0,99$. This is very surprising.

The random choice of the subsets with probability mean that we choose subsets with sizes about $\frac{n}{2}$. If the probability of choice of a subset $|A|$ is $p^{|A|} q^{n-|A|}$ then the chosen subsets have about p^n elements. A generalization (Rényi (1961b)) of Theorem 17 says that in this case we need about $m = \dfrac{\log n}{H(p, 1-p)}$ tests. (Compare with Theorem 11.)

Again, the next problem was proposed and solved by Rényi (1961b): It may occur that our tests are not reliable. The result of a test is right and false with probability β and $1-\beta$, respectively (obviously these cases are independent from the results of the other tests). In this case we need about $\dfrac{\log n}{1 - H(\beta, 1-\beta)}$

tests to identify the unknown element. (There are strong connections with Gallager's random coding (1968).)

For further generalizations see Rényi (1961b) and (1965).

Finally, we wish to mention a result of Rényi (1970) which appeared after his tragic death. A q-regular strategy is a strategy which divides into exactly q parts the subset which is known to include the unknown element $((A\alpha)(B\alpha)(C\alpha)(D\alpha))$. It is easy to see, that in this case $n \equiv 1 \pmod{q-1}$. Rényi determined the number $C_q(n)$ of different (they are not different if they differ only in the permutations of the elements $x_1, \ldots, x_n$) q-regular strategies:

$$C_q(n) = \frac{(kq)!}{k!n!} \quad \text{where} \quad n = k(q-1)+1 .$$

Similarly, the total number $D(n)$ of different strategies for $X = \{x_1, \ldots, x_n\}$ is

$$D(n) = \frac{1}{n} \sum_{k=1}^{n-1} \binom{n-2}{k-1}\binom{n+k-1}{k} \sim \frac{\sqrt{3-2\sqrt{2}}}{4\sqrt{\pi}} \frac{(3+2\sqrt{2})^n}{n^{3/2}}$$

(See also Rényi (1969)). Recently, Chorneyko and Mohanty have a generalization of these results.

5. OPEN PROBLEMS

Comparing the several sections and combining their conditions it is easy to obtain a large number of open problems. We want to emphasize some of them (it does not mean they are the most important ones, they are the most interesting only for the author):

1. Generalize the Huffman algorithm for the case $(A\gamma)$. More exactly: There are given probabilities $p(A)$ for any $A \subset X = \{x_1,...,x_n\}$ of the event that A is the set of defective elements.

A <u>general strategy</u> is a strategy which is able to determine all the defective elements. Find an algorithm which determines the general strategy with the minimal average number. (See Theorem 2, case $(A\gamma)$ and the beginning of $(A\beta)$.)

2. Find conditions under which it is possible to determine the optimal average length (see Theorems 3,4,5 and 6).

3. Generalize the results for alphabetical codes (see Theorems 9, 3, 4, 5 and 6).

4. Generalize the Huffman algorithm for the case if we can use only subsets with size $\leq k$ $\left(k<\frac{n}{2}\right)$ (see Theorems 10 and 11).

5. Determine the best strategy for Steinhaus's problem, or at least to give a better lower bound (see (3.26)).

6. Determine the minimal number m for which there exists a separating system $A_1,\ldots,A_m$ satisfying $|A_i|\leq k$ ($i=1,\ldots,m$, k fixed $<\frac{n}{2}$). Theorem 11 gives good estimation for this minimum. Generalize (3.28) for the case $(D\beta)$ when $A_1,\ldots,A_m$ are partitions into r parts and the sizes of the first $r-1$ parts are bounded. (*)

7. Determine the minimal number m for which there exists a completely separating system $A_1,\ldots,A_m$ satisfying $|A_i|\leq k$ ($i=1,\ldots,m$ k fixed $<\frac{n}{2}$). (See Theorem 12).

8. Determine the minimal number m for which there exists a system $A_1,\ldots,A_m \subset X$ such that for any x_i, x_j ($i\neq j$)) there are disjoint A_k and A_l ($A_k \cap A_l = 0$) with $x_i \in A_k$, $x_j \in A_l$.

9. Determine the maximal m for which there are subsets $A_1,\ldots,A_m$ such that any r different of them are qualitative independent (none of the sets of type $A_{i_1}, \bar{A}_{i_2} \ldots A_{i_r}$ are empty). (See the end of case $(A\alpha)(B\beta)(C\beta)(D\alpha)(E\alpha)=(E\beta)$).

10. Find a better estimation than (3.29) (see also problem 1).

11. Generalize Theorem 15 for a "three-arm balance" which has three equally sized arms (with angles $2\pi/3$), and which is balanced only if three equal weights are weighed.

12. $X=\{x_1,\ldots,x_n\}$. There is exactly one defective element. It is x_i with probability p_i. We can test any sub

---

(*) Very recently it is solved by Zs. Baranyai (b).

set $A \subset X$ whether $x_i \in A$ or not. The next test may depend on the results of the previous tests (Case $(A\alpha)(B\alpha)(C\alpha)(D\alpha)$). However the tests are noisy, that is, we receive the contrary result with probability q. Find an algorithm which determines the strategy which has the minimal average length, but decovers the defective element with given probability $1 - \varepsilon$.

(In the language of codes: variable length (not block) code with minimal code length with error probability ε.)

13. There are exactly one defective element and one mediocre element in the set X, with probabilities $p_1, \ldots, p_n$ and $q_1, \ldots, q_n$. Which strategy minimize the maximal number of test needed to indentify both elements (see the end of $(A\beta)(B\alpha)(C\alpha)(D\alpha)(E\alpha)$, and Theorem 14).

REFERENCES

BARANYAI, Zs. (a): To be published later.

(b): To be published later.

BELLMAN, R. and GLUSS, B. (1961): On Various Versions of the Defective Coin Problem. Inf. and Control, 4 118-131.

BOSE, R.C. and NELSON, R.I. (1961): A Sorting Problem, Case Institute of Technology, Computing Center, Report No. 1043, p. 1-22.

CAIRNS, S.S. (1963): Balance Scale Sorting. Amer. Math. Monthly, 70, 136-148.

CAMPBELL, L.L. (1968): Note on the connection between search theory and coding theory, Proc. of the Colloq. on Information Theory, ed. by A. Rényi, Janos Bolyai Math. Soc., Budapest Hungary.

CANTOR, D.G. (1964): Determining a set from the cardinalities of its intersections with other sets. Canad. J. Math., 16, 94-97.

CESARI, Y. (1968): Questionnaire, codage et tris, Institute Blaise Pascal, Paris.

(1970): Optimisation des questionnaires avec contrainte de rang.

CHORNEYKO, I.Z. and MOHANTI, S.G.: On the Enumeration of Pseudo-Search Codes. (submitted to Studia Sci. Math. Hungar.)

DAVID, H.A. (1959): The Method of Paired Comparisons, Hafner Publ. Co., New York.

References

DICKSON, T.I. (1969): On a Problem Concerning Separating Systems of a Finite Set. J. Combinatorial Theory, 7, 191-196.

DORFMAN, R. (1943): The Detection of Defective Members of Large Populations. Ann. Math. Statist., 14, 436-440.

ERDOS, P. and RENYI, A. (1963): On two Problems of Information Theory, Publ. Math. Inst. Hungar. Acad. Sci., 8, 241-254.

FEINSTEIN, A. (1958): Foundations of Information Theory, McGraw-Hill, New York.

FINE, N.J. (1960): Solution EI 339. Amer. Math. Monthly, 67, 697.

FORD, L.R. and JOHNSON, S.M. (1959): A tournament problem. Amer. Math. Monthly, 66, 387-389.

GALLAGER, R.G. (1968): Information theory and reliable communication, Wiley, New York.

GILBERT, E.N. and MOORE, E.F. (1959): Variable-length Binary Encodings. Bell System Techn. J., 38, 933-967.

HADRIAN, A. (1969): Optimality properties of Various Procedures for Ranking Different Numbers Using Only Binary Comparisons. Tech. Rept. No. 117. Dept. of Stat. Univ. of Minnesota.

and SOBEL, M. (1969): Selecting the th Largest of Items Using Binary Comparisons. Tech. Rept. No. 121, Dept. of Stat., Univ. of Minnesota.

(1970): Ordering the Largest Items Using Binary Comparisons. Combinatorial Math. and its Appl. Univ. of North Carolina, Chapel Hill, N.C.

HU, T.C. and TUCKER, A.C. (1970): Optimum Binary Search Trees. Combinatorial Math. and its Appl. Univ. of North Carolina, Chapel Hill, N.C.

References

HUFFMAN, D.A. (1952): A Method for the Construction of Minimum Redundancy Codes. Proc. I.R.E., 40, 1098.

KATONA, G. (1966): On Separating Systems of a Finite Set. J. Combinatorial Theory, 1, 174-194.

and LEE, M.A.: Some Remarks on the Construction of Optimal Codes (submitted to Acta Math. Acad. Sci. Hungar.)

KISLICYN, S.S. (1964): On the Selection of th Element of an Ordered Set of Pairwise Comparison (Russian). Sibirks. Math. Z., 5, 557-564.

KNUTH, D.E. (1971): Optimal Binary Search Treos, Acta Informatica, 1, 14-25.

KUMAR, S. (1970) Group-Testing to Classify All Units in a Trinomial Sample, Studia Sci. Math Hungar. 5, 229-247.

LINDSTRÖM, B. (1964): On a Combinatorial Detection Problem I. Publ. Math. Inst. Hungar. Acad. Sci., 9, 195-206.

(1966): On a Combinatorial Detection Problem II. Studia Sci. Math. Hungar., 1, 353-361.

(1965): On a Combinatorial Problem in Number Theory, Canad. Math. Bull., 8, 477-490.

MOON, J.W. (1968): Topics on Tournaments. Holt, Reinhart and Winston, New York (p. 48.).

PICARD, C. (1965): Théorie des Questionnaires. Gauthier-Villars, Paris.

RENYI, A. (1961a): On Random Generating Elements of a Finite Boolean Algebra. Acta. Sci. Math. (Szeged), 22, 75-81.

(1961b): On a Problem of Information Theory. Publ. Math. Inst. Hungar. Acad. Sci., 6, 505-516.

(1962a): Statistical Laws of Accumulation of Information. Bull, Inst. Internat. Stat., 39, (2) 311-316.

(1962b): Az informacio-akkumulacio statisztikus torvényszeruségérol. (Hungarian). Magyar Tud. Akad. III. Oszt. Kozl., 12, 15–33.

(1965): On the Theory of Random Search. Bull. Amer. Math. Soc., 71, 809–828.

(1969): Lectures on the Theory of Search. Mimeo Series No. 600.7. Dept. of Stat. Univ. of North Carolina, Chapel Hill.

(1970): On the Enumeration of Search-Codes. Acta Math. Acad. Sci. Hungar., 21, 27–33

(1971): Foundations of Probability. Holden-Day, San Francisco.

SANDELIUS, M. (1961): On an optimal search procedure. Amer. Math. Monthly, 68, 138–154.

SCHREIER, J. (1932): On tournament elimination system. (Polish). Mathesis Polska, 7, 154–160.

SHAPIRO, H.S. (1960): Problem E 1399. Amer. Math. Monthly, 67, 82.

SLUPECKI, J. (1949–51): On the system of tournaments. Colloq. Math., 2, 286–290.

SMITH, C.A.B. (1947): The counterfeit coin problem. Math. Gaz. 31, 31–39.

SOBEL, M. (1960): Group testing to classify efficiently all defectives in a binomial sample. A contribution in Information and Decision Processes, Ed. by Robert E. Machol, McGraw-Hill, 127–161.

(1967): Optimal Group Testing. Proc. of the Colloq. on Information Theory, Bolyai Math. Society, Debrecen, Hungary.

(1968a): On the ordering of the best of items using binary comparisons. Tech. Rept. No. 113. Dept. of Stat. Univ. of Minnesota. Submitted for publication.

References

(1968b): Binomial and Hypergeometric Group-Testing. Studia Sci. Math. Hungar., 3, 19-42.

(1970): A Characterization of Binary Codes that Correspond to a Class of Group-Testing Procedures. Univ. of Minnesota, Dept. of Stat. Tech. Rept. No. 148,

and GROLL, P.A. (1959): Group testing to eliminate efficiently all defectives in a binomial sample. Bell System Tech. J., 38, 1179-1252.

(1966): Binomial group-testing with unknown proportion of defectives. Technometrics, 8, 631-656.

SOBEL, M. and KUMAR, S. (1971a): Finding a Single Defective in Binomial Group-Testing. Accepted for publication in JASA.

(1971b): Group-Testing with a most tests for Finite and Univ. of Minnesota, Dept. of Statistics. Tech. Rept. No. 146.

SPERNER, E. (1928): Ein Satz über Untermengen einer endlichen Menge. Mathematische Zeitschrift. 27, 544-548.

SPENCER, J. (1970): Minimal Completely Separating Systems. J. Combinatorial Theory, 8, 466-447.

STEINHAUS, H. (1950): Mathematical Snapskost. Oxford Univ. Press., New York.

(1958): One Hundred Problem in Elementary Mathematics. (See Problems 52 and 85). Pergamon Press, London.

STERRETT, A. (1957): On the Detection of Defective Members of Large Populations. Ann. Math. Stat., 28, 1033.

UNGAR, P. (1960): The Cut-Off Point for Group Testing. Communications Pure Appl. Math., 13, 49-54.

VIGASSY, J.: personal communication.

WELLS, M.B. (1965): Application of a Language for Computing in Combinatorics. IFIP Congress.

ZIMMERMAN, S. (1959): An Optimal Search Procedure. Amer. Math. Monthly, 66, 690-693.

CONTENTS

		Page
1.	Introduction	5
2.	Connections with Noiseless Encoding	11
3.	Results	19
4.	Random Search	44
5.	Open Problems	47
	References	51

MIX
Papier aus verantwortungsvollen Quellen
Paper from responsible sources
FSC® C105338

If you have any concerns about our products,
you can contact us on
ProductSafety@springernature.com

In case Publisher is established outside the EU,
the EU authorized representative is:
**Springer Nature Customer Service Center GmbH
Europaplatz 3, 69115 Heidelberg, Germany**

Printed by Libri Plureos GmbH
in Hamburg, Germany